Pebble® Plus

## Celebrating Differences

# We All Have Different Families

by **Melissa Higgins**

Raintree is an imprint of Capstone Global Library Limited, a company incorporated in England and Wales having its registered office at 264 Banbury Road, Oxford, OX2 7DY – Registered company number: 6695582

**www.raintree.co.uk**
myorders@raintree.co.uk

Jeni Wittrock, editor; Gene Bentdahl, designer; Svetlana Zhurkin, media researcher; Kathy McColley, production specialist; Marcy Morin, studio scheduler; Sarah Schuette, photo stylist

ISBN 978 1 4747 2360 2 (hardback)
20  19  18  17  16
10 9 8 7 6 5 4 3 2 1

ISBN 978 1 4747 2364 0 (paperback)
21  20  19  18  17
10 9 8 7 6 5 4 3 2 1

**British Library Cataloguing in Publication Data**
A full catalogue record for this book is available from the British Library.

**Acknowledgements**
We would like to thank the following for permission to reproduce photographs: Capstone Studio: Karon Dubke, cover; Dreamstime: wavebreakmedia, 13; iStockphoto: kzenon, 11, Nathan Gleave, 5, Rosemarie Gearhart, 20–21, Vikram Raghuvanshi, 19; Shutterstock: AISPIX, 17, herjua, 8–9, Monkey Business Images, 7, 15, wavebreakmedia, 1.

We would like to thank Gail Saunders Smith, PhD and Donna Barkman, Children's Literature Specialist and Diversity Consultantant Ossining, New York for their invaluable help in the preparation of this book.

Every effort has been made to contact copyright holders of material reproduced in this book. Any omissions will be rectified in subsequent printings if notice is given to the publisher.

## Note to parents and teachers

This book describes and illustrates differences in families. The images support early readers in understanding the text. The repetition of words and phrases helps early readers to learn new words. This book also introduces early readers to subject-specific vocabulary words, which are defined in the Glossary. Early readers may need assistance to read some words and to use the Contents, Glossary, Read more and Index sections of the book.

Made in China

# Contents

# All kinds of families

My family isn't exactly like
your family. I like that.
There are all kinds of families,
just like there are all kinds
of people.

# Bigger families

My grandad, aunt and cousin live with us. I always have someone to talk to.

My foster parents helped me to fit in when I joined the family. They listen and understand.

My mum and dad are divorced.

At the weekend, I stay with

my dad and stepmum.

My stepsister and I have

fun together.

I'm glad my family
adopted me. I am right
where I belong.

# Smaller families

Gran teaches me to play the piano. Grandad tells me stories about our family.

My dad James drives me to school. My dad Mike cooks dinner. They both tuck me in at night.

Mum works hard, but she always has time for me. She is my favourite person in the world.

# My family

Families are made up
of people who love
each other. We take care
of each other too.

# Glossary

**adopt** legally become the parent of someone else's child

**aunt** sister of your mum or dad; an aunt can also be the wife of your uncle

**cousin** your aunt or uncle's child

**divorced** not married anymore

**foster parents** parents who bring up children who are not related to them

**stepmum** your dad's new wife

**stepsister** daughter of your step-parent

# Read more

*Emily and Patch* (City Farm), Jessie Williams (Curious Fox, 2013)

*Families Around the World* (Around the World), Clare Lewis (Raintree, 2014)

*Family (Say What You See)*, Rebecca Rissman (Raintree, 2013)

*Foster Parents (Families)*, Rebecca Rissman (Raintree, 2012)

*Helping Family and Friends* (I Can Make a Difference), Vic Parker (Raintree, 2012)

*The Most Precious Present in the World*, Becky Edwards (British Association for Adoption and Fostering, 2010)

# Index